Forty Centuries

תּוֹרָה יִשְׂרָאֵל

FORTY CENTURIES

Milestones in Early Jewish History

Published By
KEHOT PUBLICATION SOCIETY
770 EASTERN PARKWAY
BROOKLYN, NEW YORK 11213

by
KEHOT PUBLICATION SOCIETY
770 Eastern Parkway / Brooklyn, New York 11213
(718) 774-4000 / FAX (718) 774-2718

Order Department:
291 Kingston Avenue / Brooklyn, New York 11213
(718) 778-0226 / FAX (718) 778-4148
e-mail kehot@chabad.org

Library of Congress Cataloging-in-Publication Data
Torah ve-Yisrael : forty centuries.
Originally published: Brooklyn, N. Y. : Kehot, c1944
ISBN 0-8266-0230-4

1. Jews–History. 2. Judaism–History. 3. Tradition (Judaism)–History.
I. Title: Torah v'Yisrael
DS177.T67 1998
909' . 04924' 00202--dc21 98-4188
CIP

Printed in the United States of America

LIST OF CONTENTS

ILLUSTRATIONS

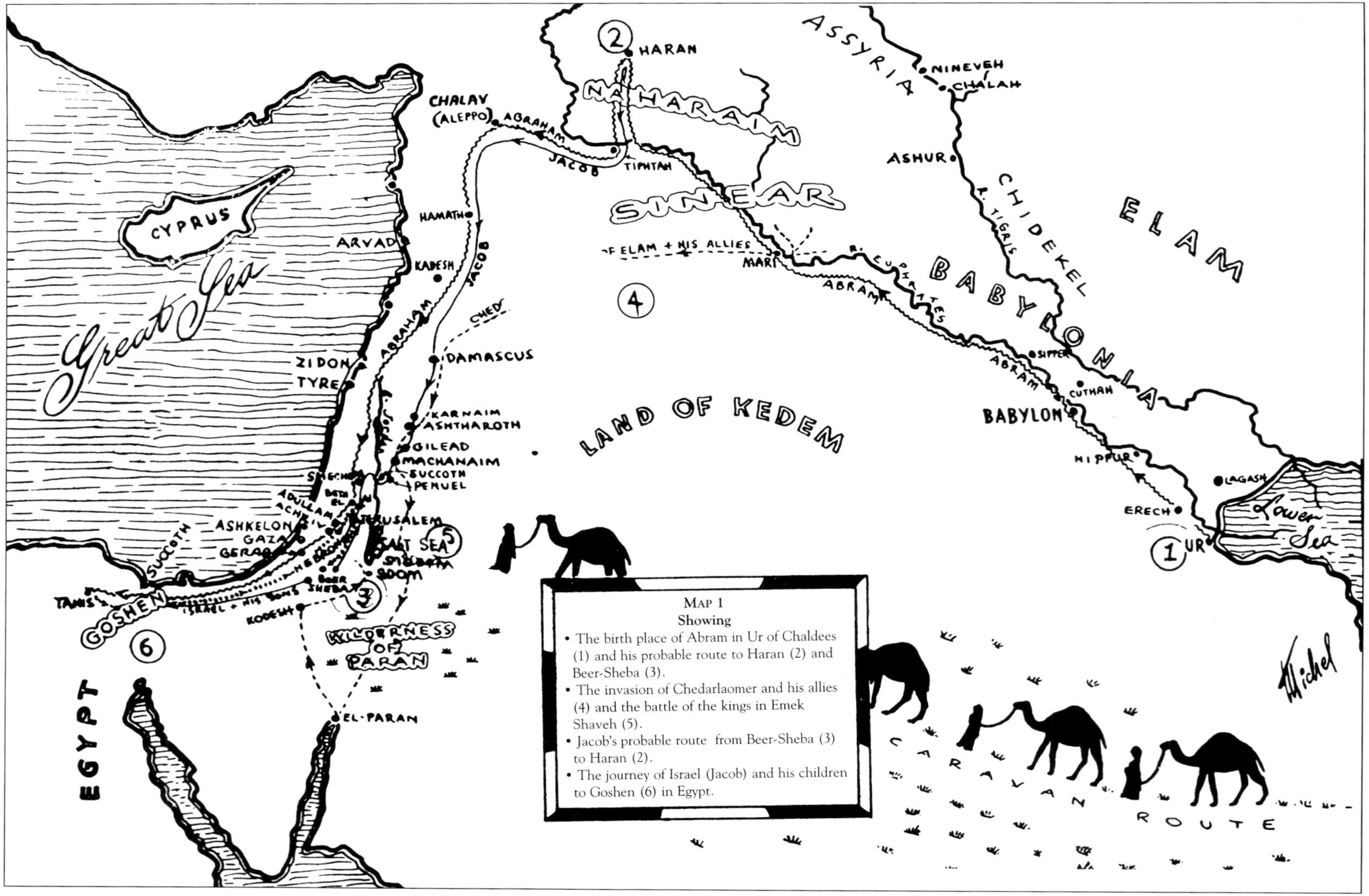

Map 1
Showing
- The birth place of Abram in Ur of Chaldees (1) and his probable route to Haran (2) and Beer-Sheba (3).
- The invasion of Chedarlaomer and his allies (4) and the battle of the kings in Emek Shaveh (5).
- Jacob's probable route from Beer-Sheba (3) to Haran (2).
- The journey of Israel (Jacob) and his children to Goshen (6) in Egypt.

MILESTONES IN EARLY JEWISH HISTORY

I.

THE history* of our people began with Abraham (1948-2123 after Creation), the first one in his generation to recognize and proclaim G-d as Creator of the Universe. At a time when all the people of the earth were idol worshippers, Abraham went forth to proclaim the unity of G-d, for which G-d made an everlasting covenant with him, that his children would be the people chosen to carry the torch of Divine wisdom and light throughout the world.

Isaac, the son and heir of Abraham and Sarah, followed in the path of his parents, and thus brought up his son Jacob (later named by G-d: Israel) who in turn taught the tradition of the family to his twelve sons, the heads of the twelve holy tribes of Israel: Reuben, Simeon, Levi, Judah, Issachar, Zebulun, Joseph, Benjamin, Dan, Naphtali, Gad and Asher.

Later, Jacob and his entire family, seventy souls in all, went down to sojourn in Egypt.

It was G-d's will that the Jewish people should in its infancy be prepared through suffering and bondage to become a spiritually and morally strong

---

* See Chronology on page 26

people. In the course of time the children of Israel grew into great numbers and were enslaved by the Egyptian Pharaohs. For 210 years the children of Israel dwelt in Egypt and despite their suffering came to number several million souls. At the height of their suffering they turned to G-d, the G-d of their fathers Abraham, Isaac and Jacob. Thereupon G-d sent them two great men, Moses and Aaron, who led them forth from Egypt, after many of G-d's wonders and miracles. The triumphant exodus of the children of Israel from Egypt took place on Nissan 15th, in the year 2448 after Creation, which we commemorate by celebrating the Freedom-festival of Pesach.

Seven weeks later (Sivan 6, 2448) G-d revealed Himself to His people on Mount Sinai, and in the presence of the entire people, amid thunder and lightning and the sound of the Shofar, proclaimed the Ten Commandments. Hence the festival of Shovuos. Thereupon Moses went up on Mt. Sinai where he stayed for forty days and forty nights, receiving the Tablets of stone upon which the Ten Commandments were written by G-d. At this time, too, he was given the entire Torah, which forms our Law, and teaches us our way of life.

Coming down from Mt. Sinai and finding that his people had set up a golden calf to worship, Moses dropped the sacred Tablets and broke them (Tammuz 17, 2448). Moses immediately destroyed the idol and made his people repent of their grave sin. On the following morning, he went up on Mt. Sinai to pray for G-d's forgiveness. Again Moses remained on Mt. Sinai for forty days and nights, until G-d told him to carve out other Tablets. Finally Moses went up on

Mt. Sinai for a third time, once again remaining there forty days and nights, coming down on the tenth of Tishri, 2449 (Yom Kippur) bringing the Tablets and the happy tidings of G-d's forgiveness.

To further assure them of forgiveness, and also, to give Israel a visible emblem of His presence among them, G-d bade Moses to erect a sanctuary. The Sanctuary was soon constructed according to the plan prescribed by G-d.

Shortly afterwards, however, the children of Israel again angered G-d. When the majority of the Spies sent by Moses to the Promised Land brought a discouraging report, saying that it was so fortified as to be unconquerable, the children of Israel refused to proceed on their way. They failed to realize that with G-d's help no obstacle was insurmountable. G-d then decreed (Av 9th, 2449), that none of that generation should live to behold the Promised Land: that they would perish in the desert in the course of forty years' wandering; only their children, the new generation, would inherit the Land.

II.

IN THE SPRING of the year 2488 the children of Israel, led by Joshua, Moses' successor, crossed the Jordan and entered the Promised Land.

During the life of Joshua and the Elders of Israel who survived him, the children of Israel were devoted to the worship of G-d and dwelt in peace.

LAND OF ISRAEL
AS DIVIDED BETWEEN
ISRAEL AND JUDAH
LEBANON MTS.
ARAM OR SYRIA
TO EUPHRATES
DAMASCUS
MOUNT HARMON
PHŒNICIA
ZAREPHATH
ASHER
WATERS OF MEROM
ASHTAROTH CARNAIM
BASHAN
NAPHTALI
KARTAN
MANASSEH
THE GREAT SEA (MEDITERRANEAN)
SEA OF CHINNERETH
ZEBULUN
MT. TABOR
CARMEL
ENDOR
HILL OF MOREH
MEGIDDO
MT. GILBOA
JEZREEL
JABESH GILEAD
MANASSEH
ISSACHAR
MAHANAIM
FOREST OF EPHRAIM
PLAIN OF SHARON
TIRZAH
JORDAN R.
COAST
SAMARIA
MT. EBAL
MT. GERIZIM
PENUEL
GAD
EPHRAIM
SUCCOTH
RAMOTH GILEAD
Jaffa
DAN
L. SHILOH
RABAT AMMON
AMMON
Great Syrian Desert
BETHEL
BENJAMIN
GILGAL
JERICHO
HESHBON
EKRON
PHILISTINE
JABNEH
GIBEA
JERUSALEM
BETHLEHEM
MT. NEBO
MADEBA
REUBEN
PHILISTIA
SHEPHELAH
MTS. OF JUDAH
KIRJATHAIM
TEKOAH
ABARIM MTS.
BEZER
JUDAH
LAGHISH
HEBRON
EN-GEDI
SALT SEA
ZIPH
TO EGYPT
ZIKLAG
BEER-SHEBA
SIMEON
MOAB
VALE OF SIDDIN
NEGEB or South Country
EDOM
AMALEKITES
SELAH (JOKTHEEL)

Later, however, the Jews fell under the influence of the neighboring heathen countries, and turned to idol worship. As soon as they turned away from the path of the Torah they found themselves oppressed by their neighbors. Under this cruel oppression they turned back to G-d with renewed faith, and G-d sent them the Judges who rallied the people and saved them from their savage neighbors. Thus the fortune of the people of Israel changed many times in the course of more than three hundred years, until G-d selected Saul, the son of Kish of the tribe of Benjamin, to be King of Israel. Later G-d transferred the crown to David, the son of Yishai (Jesse), of the tribe of Judah (2854-2924).

King Solomon (2912-2964), who succeeded his father David at the age of 12, was commanded by G-d to build the Beth Hamikdosh in Jerusalem.

After King Solomon's death only the tribes of Judah and Benjamin remained loyal to Rehaboam, Solomon's son and heir, while the other ten tribes set up a separate Kingdom with Jeroboam, the son of Nevat, as their king. Thus the Land of Israel was divided into two Kingdoms: the Northern Kingdom of the Ten Tribes, and the Southern Kingdom of Judah. (See Map).

Gradually the Jewish people turned away from the path of G-d, falling under the influence of the idolatrous and corrupt neighboring peoples. They did not heed the warnings of the holy prophets whom G-d sent to admonish and warn them of impending retribution, unless they would turn back to the Torah and the observance of its commandments. Retribu-

The (Second) Temple

בית המקדש השני

tion finally came, when the King of Assyria, invaded the Kingdom of the Ten Tribes and led them into exile, destroying their capital Samaria and ravaging their land (3205).

The Kingdom of Judah continued on, but the people did not learn of the dreadful calamity that had befallen their brethren in the north. Finally, G-d delivered them into the hands of the powerful King Nebuchadnezzar of Babylon. Nebuchadnezzar successfully invaded the Land of Israel and besieged Jerusalem (Teveth 10), capturing it after a siege of nearly three years, and destroying the Beth Hamikdosh (Av 9, 3338). The people were driven into exile into Babylon.

III.

THE BABYLONIAN exile lasted for seventy years. Toward the end of this period the great miracle of Purim occurred (Adar 14, 3405), when the Jews in the vast Persian Empire were miraculously saved from the wicked Haman.

At the end of the seventy years' exile G-d took pity upon his people and returned them to the Land of Israel. The Beth Hamikdosh was rebuilt, and the Jewish people resettled on their land. Though politically under the rule of Persia and, since Alexander the Great, under the rule of Greece and Syria, they were free to worship their G-d and observe the commandments of the Torah.

A wave of religious persecution by Antiochus, King of Syria, led to the revolt of the brave Hasmoneans, who defeated the Syrian armies and freed the Land of Israel from foreign domination ("The Miracle of Chanukah," Kislev 25, 3622).

For many years the crown was held by the priestly family of the Hasmoneans, and the Jews were free and independent. Later, however, the crown was seized by Herod the Edomite, a slave in the House of the Hasmoneans, who murdered all the members of the Hasmonean family and set up a dynasty of his own.

The Land of Israel became torn by civil war and fell under Roman domination. Hate and strife were rampant and the true leaders of the people, the Pharisees and the Tanaim, were largely ignored.

Under these circumstances a group of zealots organized a widespread revolt to free the Land of Israel from Roman oppression. Despite the warning by the religious leaders that the revolt against mighty Rome was doomed, the revolt was started. Numerous Roman legions, under the leadership of Vespasian and his son Titus then swept the land. One after another the fortresses of the Land of Israel fell under the mighty blows of the Roman armies, until Jerusalem was besieged. The incredible bravery and courage of the Jewish defenders were of no avail, and Jerusalem was captured for the second time (Tammuz 17th). The Beth Hamikdosh was destroyed (again on Av 9th, in the year of 3828), and hundreds of thousands of Jews were slain and murdered; many were taken captive to perish in slavery or fighting fierce animals in circusses. The whole of the Land of Israel was destroyed, and of the magnificent Beth Hamikdosh nothing but the western wall remained, later to be called the Wailing Wall, because of the many tears the Jews shed there through all the centuries that have since elapsed.

IV.

THE only consolation, besides the Divine Promise of Redemption, that the war-torn and suffering Jewish people found at that time, was the great Torah academy headed by Rabban Jochanan ben Zakkai in Yavneh. This great Tanna, as well as his contemporaries and successors, taught the Jewish people how to adjust themselves to their new status of a people in exile, until the time should come when G-d would gather all the dispersed Jews from the four corners of the earth and lead them back to the Land of Israel: above all, the Jews must remain loyal to G-d and to His Torah; they must worship Him through prayer and the observance of the commandments of the Torah, and carry the light of the Torah wherever Providence should direct them; they must always remember that "for our sins we have been exiled from our land," and that only through repentance and return to G-d will we be redeemed from Exile and led to our land by Messiah, our Righteous Redeemer.

* * *

The Western Wall הכותל המערבי

These teachings and our loyal adherence to our Torah and Tradition, have helped us to retain our identity in the lands of our dispersion and to survive all the inhuman persecutions to which our poor and defenseless people have been consigned. Wherever Jews sojourn, they set up academies (Yeshivoth) to study the Torah and to strengthen the foundations of our tradition and religious observance. For the Torah is our life, our refuge, our very existence.

TORAH AND MASSORAH

THE WRITTEN TORAH
PENTATEUCH, PROPHETS, HOLY WRITINGS

THE PENTATEUCH (Five Books of the Torah). Moses wrote all the Five Books of the Torah; even the passages that refer to him he wrote in the third person, for every word of it was dictated to him by G-d.

THE 613 COMMANDMENTS. The Torah relates how G-d created the universe, how the human race came into being from Adam and Eve, how our Fathers, Abraham, Isaac and Jacob fared, how the Jewish people became a nation, chosen by G-d to be 'a kingdom of priests and a holy nation' through receiving and observing the Torah. The Torah contains 613 commandments, of which 248 are positive (what to do) and 365 are negative (what not to do). The precepts and commandments cover every phase of the Jew's life, both the duties to fellow man and the way to worship G-d, in order to attain the highest moral standards.

MASSORAH—(Tradition). In addition to the precepts, commandments and prohibitions written in the Torah, G-d taught Moses more laws which he was to memorize and orally convey to his successors, who in turn were to uphold this tradition from generation to generation. Many laws and customs have thus been practiced by us traditionally, as if they were actually written in the Torah.

The PROPHETS. The books of the Prophets include: Joshua, Judges, Samuel, Kings, Jeremiah, Ezekiel, Isaiah and Tre-assar (the 12 books of the Minor Prophets: Hosea, Joel, Amos, Obadiah, Jonah, Micah, Nahum, Habakkuk, Zephaniah, Haggai, Zecharia, Malachi).

THE HOLY WRITINGS. These include the books of Ruth, Psalms, Job, Proverbs, Ecclesiastes, Song of Songs, Lamentations, Daniel, Esther, Ezra and Chronicles. All these books were written by one or another of our prophets by divine inspiration ("Ruach Hakodesh").

The books of Samuel, Kings, Ezra and Chronicles are subdivided into: Samuel I and Samuel II; Kings I and Kings II; Ezra and Nehemiah; Chronicles I and Chronicles II.

In all we had 48 prophets and 7 prophetesses whose prophecies were recorded for their everlasting importance. In addition to them there have been prophets in Israel in every generation, but because of the fact that their prophecies were confined to their times alone, they were not recorded.

שלשלת הקבלה
THE COURSE OF TRADITION

	Year after Creation	
משה	2448	Moses receives the Torah on Mount Sinai
יהושע	2488	Joshua — Elazar
פנחס, זקנים	2516	Pinehas — Elders 2516-2830, including Judges:

Othniel	till 2566	Yair	till 2764
Ehud	" 2636	Jephtah	" **2787**
Shamgar	" 2636	Avtzan (Boaz)	" 2793
Barak-Deborah	" 2676	Eilon	" 2803
Gideon and Son	" 2719	Abdon	" 2811
Tola	" 2742	Samson	" 2830

עלי	2830	Eli and his Beth-din (Court)
שמואל	2870	Samuel and his Beth-din
דוד	2884	David and his Beth-din
אחי' השילוני	2924	Achiya of Shiloh and his Beth-din
אליהו הנביא	2962	Elijah the Prophet
אלישע הנביא	3047	Elisha the Prophet
יהוידע הכהן	3055	Yehoyoda the Priest
זכרי' בנו	3070	Zechariah his son
הושע בן בארי	3090	Hoshea ben Beeri
עמוס	3110	Amos
ישעי'	3140	Isaiah
מיכה	3160	Micah
יואל	3190	Joel
נחום	3240	Nahum
חבקוק	3254	Habakuk
צפני'	3280	Zefaniah
ירמי'	3316	Jeremiah
ברוך בן נרי'	3350	Baruch ben Neriah
עזרא ואנשי כנסת הגדולה	3370	Ezra and his Beth-din (The Men of the Great Assembly: Daniel, Mordecai, Nehemia, Chananiah, Mishael, Azariah, etc.)
שמעון הצדיק	3400	Shimon Hatzadik (the Just), last of the Great Assembly
אנטיגנוס	3460	Antignos of Soho
יוסי ויוסי	3500	Jose ben Joezer and Jose ben Jochanan
יהושע ונתאי	3560	Joshua ben Prachyah and Nitai the Arbelite
יהודא ושמעון	3621	Judah ben Tabbai and Shimon ben Shotach
שמעי' ואבטליון	3722	Shemayah and Abtalyon
הלל ושמאי	3728	Hillel and Shammai
ר' שמעון	3768	Rabban Shimon ben Hillel and Rabbi Jochanan ben Zakkai
ר' גמליאל	3800	Rabban Gamliel b. Shimon and disciples of Rabbi Jochanan ben Zakkai
ר' שמעון	3810	Rabban Shimon b. Gamliel and Rabbi Akiba
ר' גמליאל	3828	Rabban Gamliel and disciples of R. Akiba
ר' שמעון	3881	Rabban Shimon b. Gamliel
רבינו הקדוש	3910	Rabbi Judah Hanassi — *Redactor of the Mishnah*
רב, שמואל, ר״י	3979	His sons R. Shimon and R. Gamliel, R. Chiyah, Rav, Samuel, R. Jochanan
רב הונא	4010	R. Huna, R. Judah, R. Nachman, R. Kahana
רבה ורב יוסף	4060	Rabba and R. Joseph
אביי ורבא	4085	Abaye and Rava
רב אשי ורבינא	4127	Rav Ashi and Ravina
חתימת התלמוד	4260	*Completion of Talmud* through R. Ashi, Ravina and their disciples

משה קבל תורה מסיני ומסרה . . .
(אבות א: א)

Moses received the Torah on Mt. Sinai and handed it down . . .
(ABOTH I:1)

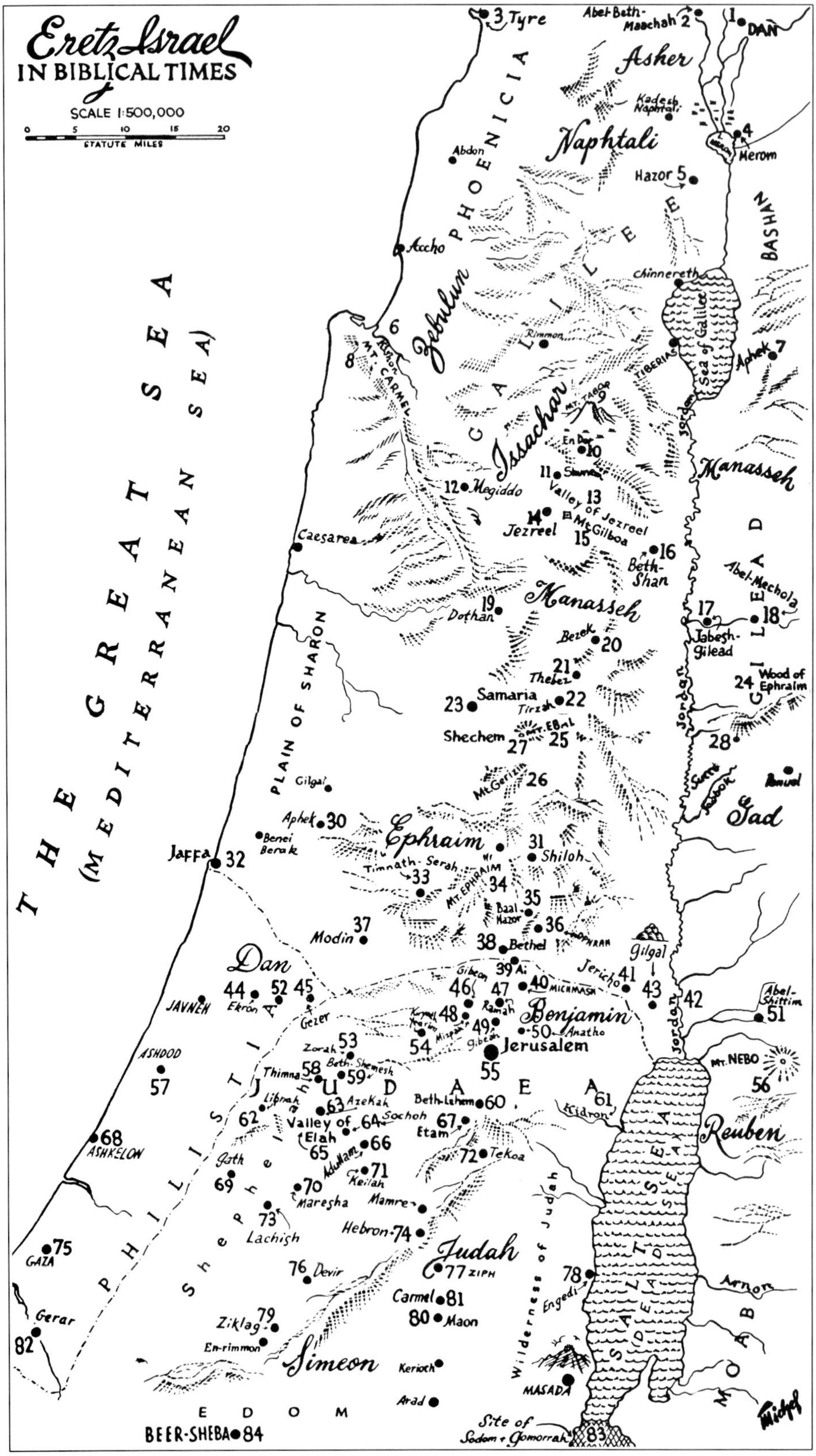
Eretz Israel
IN BIBLICAL TIMES
SCALE 1:500,000
0 5 10 15 20
STATUTE MILES
THE GREAT SEA
(MEDITERRANEAN SEA)
PHOENICIA
GALILEE
BASHAN
GILEAD
PLAIN OF SHARON
JUDAEA
PHILISTIA
Shephelah
EDOM
MOAB
SALT SEA
DEAD SEA
Sea of Galilee
Jordan
Asher
Naphtali
Zebulun
Issachar
Manasseh
Ephraim
Gad
Dan
Benjamin
Reuben
Judah
Simeon
3 Tyre
Abel-Beth-Maachah 2
1 DAN
Kadesh Naphtali
4 Merom
Abdon
Hazor 5
Accho
Chinnereth
6
8
MT. CARMEL
Kishon
Rimmon
TIBERIAS
Aphek 7
MT. TABOR 9
En Dor 10
11 Shunem
12 Megiddo
Valley of Jezreel
13
14 Jezreel
Mt. Gilboa
15
16 Beth-Shan
Caesarea
Abel-Mechola
17
18
Jabesh-Gilead
19 Dothan
Bezek 20
21 Thebez
24 Wood of Ephraim
23 Samaria
Tirzah 22
Shechem 27
MT. EBAL 25
28
Mt. Gerizim 26
Gilgal
Penuel
Aphek 30
Benei Berak
Jaffa 32
31 Shiloh
Timnath-Serah 33
MT. EPHRAIM
34
35
Baal-Hazor
36
Modin 37
38 Bethel
Gilgal
39 Ai
Jericho 41
43
42
44
52
45
JAVNEH
Ekron
Gezer
Gibeon
46
47
40 MICHMASH
Ramah
48
Kiryat Yearim
49
Mizpah
Gibeah
50 Anatho
Abel-Shittim 51
ASHDOD
57
Zorah 53
Beth-Shemesh
54
Jerusalem
55
MT. NEBO
56
Thimna 58
59
Libnah
62
63 Azekah
Beth-Lehem 60
61
Kidron
Valley of Elah
64 Sochoh
65
66
Adullam
67
Etam
68
ASHKELON
Gath
69
71 Keilah
70
72 Tekoa
Maresha
Mamre
73 Lachish
Hebron 74
75 GAZA
76 Devir
77 ZIPH
78 Engedi
Wilderness of Judah
Arnon
Gerar
82
Carmel 81
80 Maon
Ziklag 79
En-rimmon
Kerioth
MASADA
Arad
BEER-SHEBA 84
Site of Sodom + Gomorrah 83
Michel

Legend

1. DAN – Northernmost city. Calf worship instituted by Jeroboam.
2. ABEL-BETH-MAACHAH – Sheba's head was thrown to Joab.
3. TYRE – Hiram, king of Tyre, helped Solomon build the Beth Hamikdosh.
4. MEROM – Canaanite chiefs, under Jabin king of Hazor, defeated by Joshua.
5. HAZOR – See 4. Sisera, captain of Jabin, defeated by Barak and Deborah.
6. BROOK OF KISHON – Scene of Sisera's defeat. Prophets of Baal slain by Elijah's command.
7. APHEK – Ahab defeated Benhadad of Syria.
8. MT. CARMEL – Elijah's contest with false prophets.
9. MT. TABOR – Barak charged upon Sisera from this mountain. Gideon's brothers slain here.
10. EN DOR – Saul consulted a witch.
11. SHUNEM – Elisha revived child of Shunemite woman.
12. MEGIDDO – Ahaziah of Judah mortally wounded by Jehu. (Site of extensive modern excavations.)
13. VALLEY OF JEZREEL – Gideon with 300 men defeated vast Midianite army.
14. JEZREEL – Built by Ahab. Naboth's vineyard.
15. MT. GILBOA – Philistine victory over Saul.
16. BETH-SHAN – Bodies of King Saul and his sons rescued by the people of Jabesh-Gilead.
17. JABESH-GILEAD – See 16. Saul defeated Ammonites besieging the city. Bodies of King Saul and his sons buried here.
18. ABEL-MECHOLAH – Birthplace of the prophet Elisha.
19. DOTHAN – Where Joseph was sold by his brothers.
20. BEZEK – Canaanite stronghold captured after Joshua's death.
21. THEBEZ – Abimelech killed when a woman threw a millstone upon his head.
22. TIRZAH – First capital of Northern Kingdom.
23. SAMARIA – Second capital of Northern Kingdom, built by Omri. Captured by Assyrians under Shalmaneser.
24. WOOD OF EPHRAIM – Absalom, son of King David, Killed by Joab.
25. MT. EBAL – "Mountain of the Curse."
26. MT. GERIZIM – "Mountain of the Blessings." Jotham proclaimed his parable from this height to the people of Shechem.
27. SHECHEM – Joshua bade farewell to the tribes of Israel. Abimelech proclaimed king (see 21). Jeroboam elected king. Division of the Kingdom.
28. SUCCOTH – People refused to aid Gideon in battle against Midianites, and were severely punished after his victory (see 13).
29. PENUEL – Where Jacob wrestled with angel. People refused to aid Gideon (see 28).
30. APHEK – Israelites defeated by Philistines; Holy Ark captured.
31. SHILOH – Seat of Sanctuary. Eli the High Priest brought up Samuel.
32. JAFFA – Jonah boarded ship for Tarshish.
33. TIMNATH SERAH – Burial place of Joshua.
34. MT. EPHRAIM – Dwelling place of Deborah.
35. BAAL-HAZOR – David's son Abalsom had large flocks grazing here.
36. OPHRA – Dwelling place of Gideon.
37. MODIN – Birthplace of the Maccabees.
38. BETHEL – Scene of Jacob's dream. Jeroboam instituted calf worship, denounced here by prophet Amos many years later.
39. AI – Second Canaanite stronghold captured by Joshua.
40. MICHMASH – Scene of Jonathan's exploits against the Philistines.
41. JERICHO – First stronghold captured by Joshua.
42. JORDAN – Approximate place where Israelites crossed the river entering the Promised Land.
43. GILGAL – First camp of Israelites in Promised Land.
44. EKRON – Philistine stronghold.
45. GEZER – Captured by Joshua. David defeated Philistines. (Scene of modern excavations.)
46. GIBEON – Gibeonites sued for peace. Joshua defeated Canaanite army. Seat of Sanctuary. G-d appeared unto Solomon in a dream.
47. RAMAH – Birthplace of the prophet Samuel.
48. MIZPAH – Samuel summoned the people for day of prayer.
49. GIBEAH – King Saul's capital.
50. ANATHOTH – Birthplace of Jeremiah.
51. ABEL-SHITTIM – Last camp of Israel before crossing the Jordan.
52. GIBBETHON – During siege of city held by Philistines, King Elah of Israel murdered by Zimri.
53. ZORAH – Birthplace of Samson.
54. KIRYATH-YEARIM – Holy Ark held here until it was moved by David.
55. JERUSALEM – Captured by King David. Capital of Judea. Seat of Beth Hamikdosh. Destroyed by Babylonians (3338) and by Romans (3828). The Holy City, may G-d rebuild and restore it to its glory.
56. MT. NEBO – From here Moses saw the Promised Land: died here.
57. ASHDOD – Philistine stronghold. Captured Holy Ark, placed in temple of Dagon, quickly released.
58. THIMNAH – Samson's exploits.
59. BETH-SHEMESH – Joash of Israel defeated Amaziah of Judah.
60. BETH-LEHEM – Birthplace of David.
61. BROOK OF KIDRON – David passed it in flight from Absalom.
62. LIBNAH – Canaanite city captured by Joshua.
63. AZEKAH – One of last three cities captured by Babylonians.
64. SOCHOH – Philistines encamped near here with Goliath.
65. VALLEY OF ELAH – Saul's army faced Philistines; David slew Goliath.
66. ADULLAM – David hid in a cave nearby, in flight from Saul.
67. ETAM – Samson concealed himself in a cave nearby.
68. ASHKELON – Philistine stronghold.
69. GATH – Philistine stronghold. ("Tell it not in Gath, proclaim it not in the streets of Ashkelon.")
70. MARESHAH – Asa defeated Zerah the Ethiopian who invaded Judah with a million warriors. Birthplace of the prophet Micah.
71. KEILAH – David rescued city from Philistines.
72. TEKOA – Birthplace of Prophet Amos.
73. LACHISH – Captured by Joshua. Amaziah of Judah slain in rebellion.
74. HEBRON – Cave of Machpelah.
75. GAZA – Samson escaped with gates of the city. Captured from Philistines by King Hezekiah.
76. DEVIR – Captured by Joshua.
77. ZIPH – David sought refuge here in flight from Saul, betrayed by them.
78. ENGEDI – Where David cut off the skirt of King Saul.
79. ZIKLAG – Used by David as base for operations against Amalekites.
80. MAON – Visited by David in flight from Saul.
81. CARMEL – Home of Nabal. David married Abigail.
82. GERAR – Ancient Philistine city visited by Isaac.
83. DEAD SEA – Site of Sodom and Gomorrah.
84. BEER-SHEBA – Dwelling place of the Patriarchs. Southernmost city. David took a census from "Dan to Beer-Sheba."

THE ORAL LAW

THIS includes all that Moses learnt from G-d by heart which he did not write down, but transmitted orally to his successors. This tradition passed on from generation to generation in the following order:* Moses handed it down to Joshua, Joshua to the Elders, the Elders to the Prophets, the Prophets to the Men of the Great Synagogue (at the time of the Babylonian Exile). One of the last Men of the Great Synagogue was Simon the Just (he was also High Priest in the Second Temple), and he handed the tradition down to Antigonos of Soho. The Oral Torah was further handed down by tradition in the following order: Jose, the son of Joezer and Jose son of Jochanan—Joshua son of Perachaya and Nittai the Arbelite—Judah ben Tabbai and Simeon ben Shettach.—Shemayah and Abtalyon—Hillel (Hazaken, the First) and Shammai—Rabban Jochanan ben Zakkai and Rabban Simeon son of Hillel—Rabban Gamliel (Hazaken) son of Rabban Simeon.—Rabbi Akiba and Rabban Simeon, son of Gamliel—Rabban Gamliel, Rabbi Simeon son of Jochoi, Rabbi Meir, Rabbi Judah, etc.—Rabban Simeon son of Rabban Gamliel—Rabbi Judah Hanassi (son of Rabban Simeon) known as Rabbenu Hakadosh (Our Holy Rabbi), or just "Rabbi."

MISHNAH. From Moses until Rabbenu Hakadosh the traditional laws were thus learnt by heart and handed down from generation to generation orally. Rabbenu Hakadosh, however, realizing that because of growing hardships and persecutions the Jews

* See "The Course of Tradition" on page 17

might not be able to retain by memory all these traditional laws, decided to record them. Being both a great scholar and a man of considerable means, he gathered around him the greatest scholars of his time and recorded all the traditional laws and interpretations of the Torah that they had learnt from their teachers. All this vast knowledge he arranged into six sections: 1. Zeraim—"Seeds"—agricultural laws; 2. Moed—"Season"—laws of Sabbath and Festivals; 3. Nashim—"Women"—marriage laws; 4. Nezikin—"Damages"—civil and criminal laws; 5. Kodshim—"Holy Things"—laws on Sacrifices; and 6. Taharoth — "Purities" — laws of cleanliness and purity. Each section was further subdivided into tractates (Mesichtoth): each tractate into chapters and each chapter into Mishnayoth. **

GEMARA. The Mishnayoth were written down very concisely, without discussion or much argumentation. "Rabbi's" disciples later compiled the "Toseftoth" and "Brayetoth" where the subjects of the Mishnayoth are examined at greater length. The great scholars living after the redaction and completion of the Mishnah, who studied, examined, discussed and interpreted the Mishnayoth, were called 'Amoraim' (meaning 'teachers' or 'interpreters'). Thus the Mishnayoth were studied in the great Yeshivoth of Eretz Israel and Babylon for about 400 years after the destruction of the Second Temple. Finally, Rav Ashi, one of the greatest scholars of his time, a man combining both scholarship and wealth, realizing that

** See complete list of names of the Tractates of the Mishnah in Pocket Encyclopedia 5704.

the growing troubles and sufferings of the Jewish people might cause many of the laws and interpretations, which had been handed down traditionally for many generations, to be forgotten, decided to write them down. Together with his contemporary, Ravina, and other heads of the Yeshivoth in Babylon, they gathered and compiled the Gemara—the Talmud Bably, which Jews hold sacred and study to this very day. The scholars of Eretz Israel had already compiled and arranged the Talmud Jerushalmi, which is also held sacred and studied by our scholars to this day.

RABBANAN SEBURAI. The scholars who lived after the redaction of the Gemara, were known as Rabbanan Seburai (Rabbis - interpreters). They subtracted nothing from the Talmud; they merely interpreted the Gemara.

GEONIM. The great scholars, successors to the Rabbanan Seburai, were called Geonim. (Gaon—excellency). For many years they headed the great Babylonian academies. The last one of them was Rav Hai Gaon.

RISHONIM AND ACHARONIM ("Earlier" and "latter" codifiers). After the Geonim lived the great scholars: Rabbenu Chananel, Rabbi Isaac Alfasi, Rabbi Joseph ibn Migash, Rashi, Rambam (Maimonides) and others. Rashi (Rabbi Solomon Itzchaki) won immortal fame by his commentaries on the Torah and Talmud, without which it would now be almost impossible to understand either; and Maimonides—by his Mishneh-Torah ("Repetition of the Law")—a codification of all the laws of Israel. The grandsons of Rashi together with other great scholars of their time compiled the "Tosefoth" (commentaries on the Talmud).

Various great scholars of later years gathered the final decisions and settlements of disputed laws, as codified by the 'Rishonim' and arranged them. The most outstanding of them was: the 'Author of the Turim' (Rabbi Jacob son of the 'Rosh'—Rabbi Osher son of Rabbi Jechiel). Later, Rabbi Joseph, son of Rabbi Ephraim Caro, reexamined and recast the law-decisions and arranged them in his famous work the Shulchan-aruch ("Table arranged"), so that every Jew could learn and understand them.

* * *

THE HOLY TORAH—the Written Torah and the Oral Torah—is the divine gift that G-d has given us through Moses, on Mount Sinai. This selfsame Torah was handed down by Moses to his successor Joshua, and so on from generation to generation to the present day. As G-d is eternal, so the Torah which He has given is eternal, and through studying the Torah and observing the precepts and commandments of the Torah, the Jewish people are also eternal.

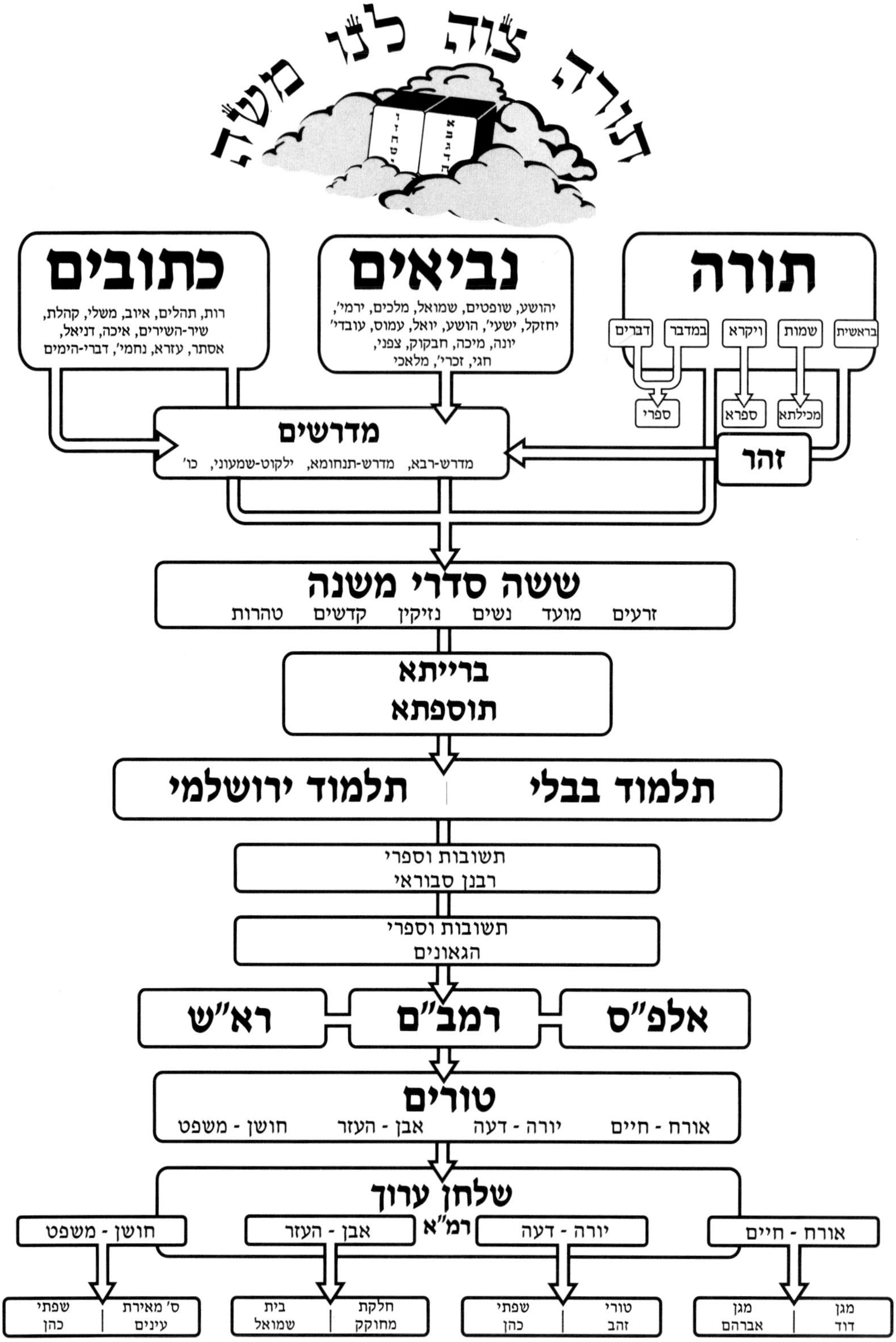

וְזֹאת הַתּוֹרָה אֲשֶׁר שָׂם מֹשֶׁה לִפְנֵי בְּנֵי יִשְׂרָאֵל

מקרא משנה תלמוד ואגדה אפילו מה שתלמיד ותיק עתיד להורות לפני רבו כבר נאמר למשה בסיני" (תלמוד ירושלמי פאה ב:ד)

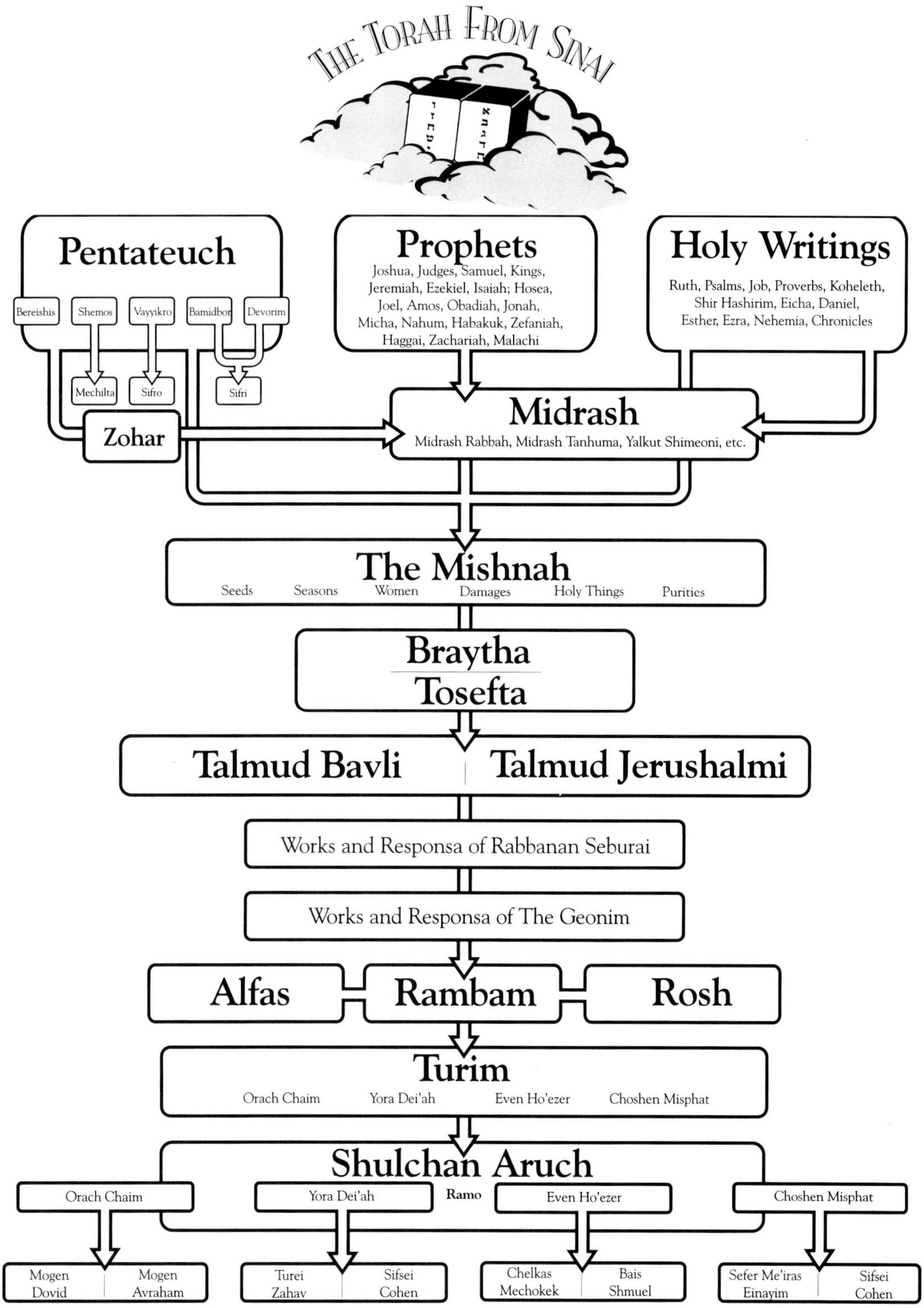

"The Torah which Moses commanded us is an inheritance of the congregation of Jacob" (Deuteronomy 33:4)

מקרא משנה תלמוד ואגדה אפילו מה שתלמיד ותיק עתיד להורות
לפני רבו כבר נאמר למשה בסיני" (תלמוד ירושלמי פאה ב׳:ד׳)

Some Outstanding Events in Jewish History

Event	Year after creation
G-d created Adam and Eve on the sixth day after the creation of the world	
Adam died, 930 years old	930
Noach	1056-2006
The Flood	1656
Abraham	1948-2123
Isaac	2048-2228
Jacob	2108-2255
The Children of Israel in Egypt (in bondage)	2238-2448
Moses	2368-2488
The Exodus from Egypt	2448
The Revelation on Mount Sinai and The Giving of the Torah	2448
The wandering of the Jews in the Desert	2448-2488
The Jews enter Eretz Yisroel	2488
King David	2854-2924
King Solomon	2912-2964
Erection of the First Holy Temple	2928
Death of Solomon. Division of the land into two kingdoms: Judah (Tribes of Judah and Benjamin) and Israel (remaining ten tribes)	2964
End of the Kingdom of the Ten Tribes	3205
Destruction of the First Holy Temple	3338
Babylonian Exile	3338-3408
The Miracle of Purim	3404-3405
Erection of the Second Holy Temple	3408
The Miracle of Chanukah	3622
Destruction of the Second Temple	3828

Event	Date
Redaction of the Mishnah	(about) 4000
Redaction of the Babylonian Talmud	(about) 4260
Rabbanan Seburai	4260-4300
Geonim	4349-4798
Rav Saadiah Gaon	4642-4702
Rav Hai Gaon	4699-4798
Rabbi Isaac Alfassi—"Rif"	4773-4863
Rabbi Solomon Itzchaki—"Rashi"	4800-4865
Rabbi Jacob ben Meir (Rabbenu Tam) of the chief authors of Tosefoth	4860-4931
Rabbi Moses ben Maimon—"Rambam" or Maimonides	4895-4964
Rabbi Moses ben Nachman—"Ramban" or Nachmanides	4954-5029
Rabbi Solomon ben Abraham ibn Adreth—"Rashba"	4995-5070
Rabbi Osher ben Yechiel—"Rosh"	About 5010-5087
Rabbi Jacob (his son) "Baal HaTurim"	About 5029-5100
Rabbi Joseph Caro—"Baal Ha-Shulchan Aruch"	5248-5335
Expulsion from Spain	5252
Rabbi Moses Issereles—"Remo"	5280-5332
Rabbi Isaac Luriah—"Ari"	5294-5332

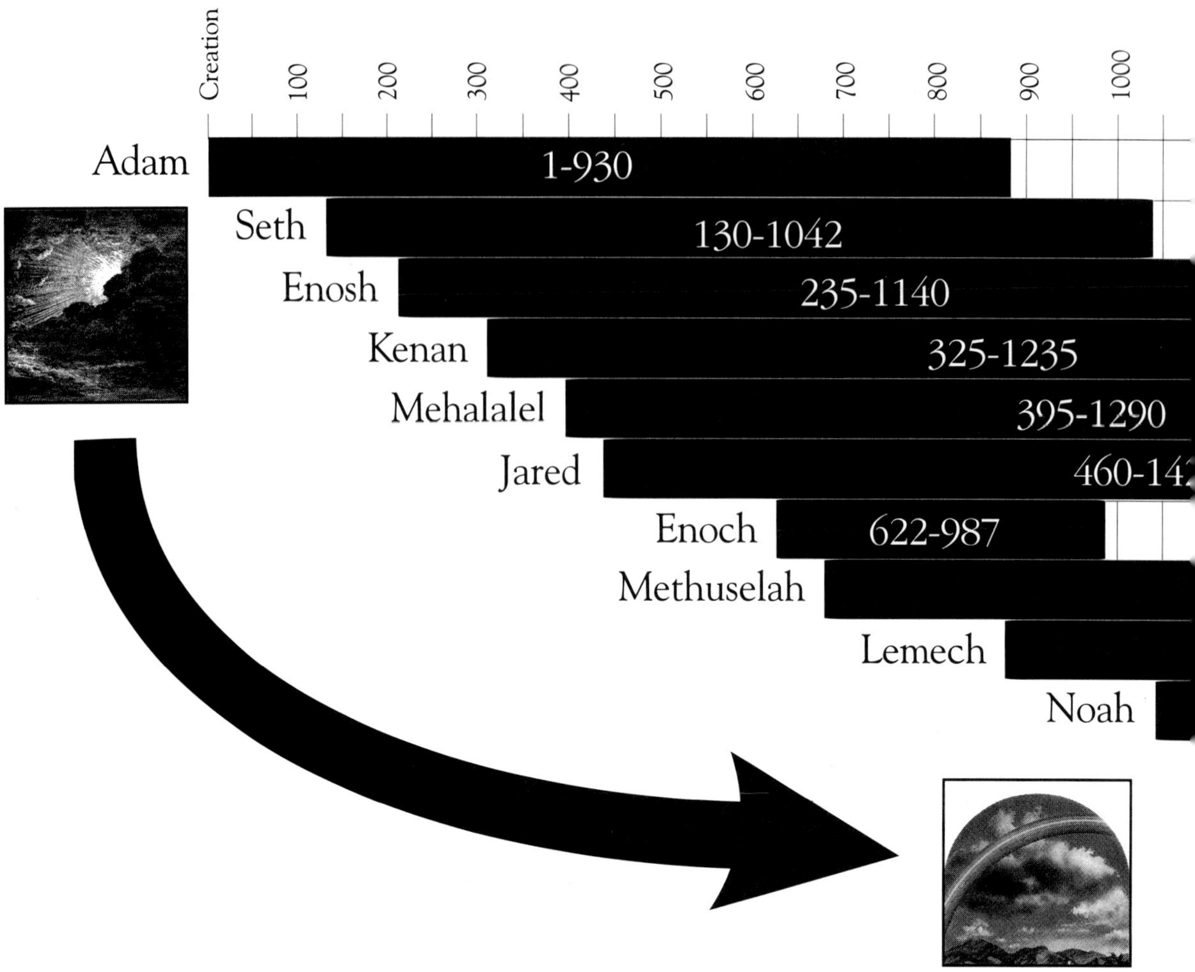

From Creation to Mount Sinai

Chart showing twenty–six generations from the creation of the world to the giving of the Torah on Mount Sinai in the year 2448 after the Creation.

It will be seen from the chart that Adam, Methuselah, Shem, Jacob, Amram and Moses lived long enough to see one another in succession.

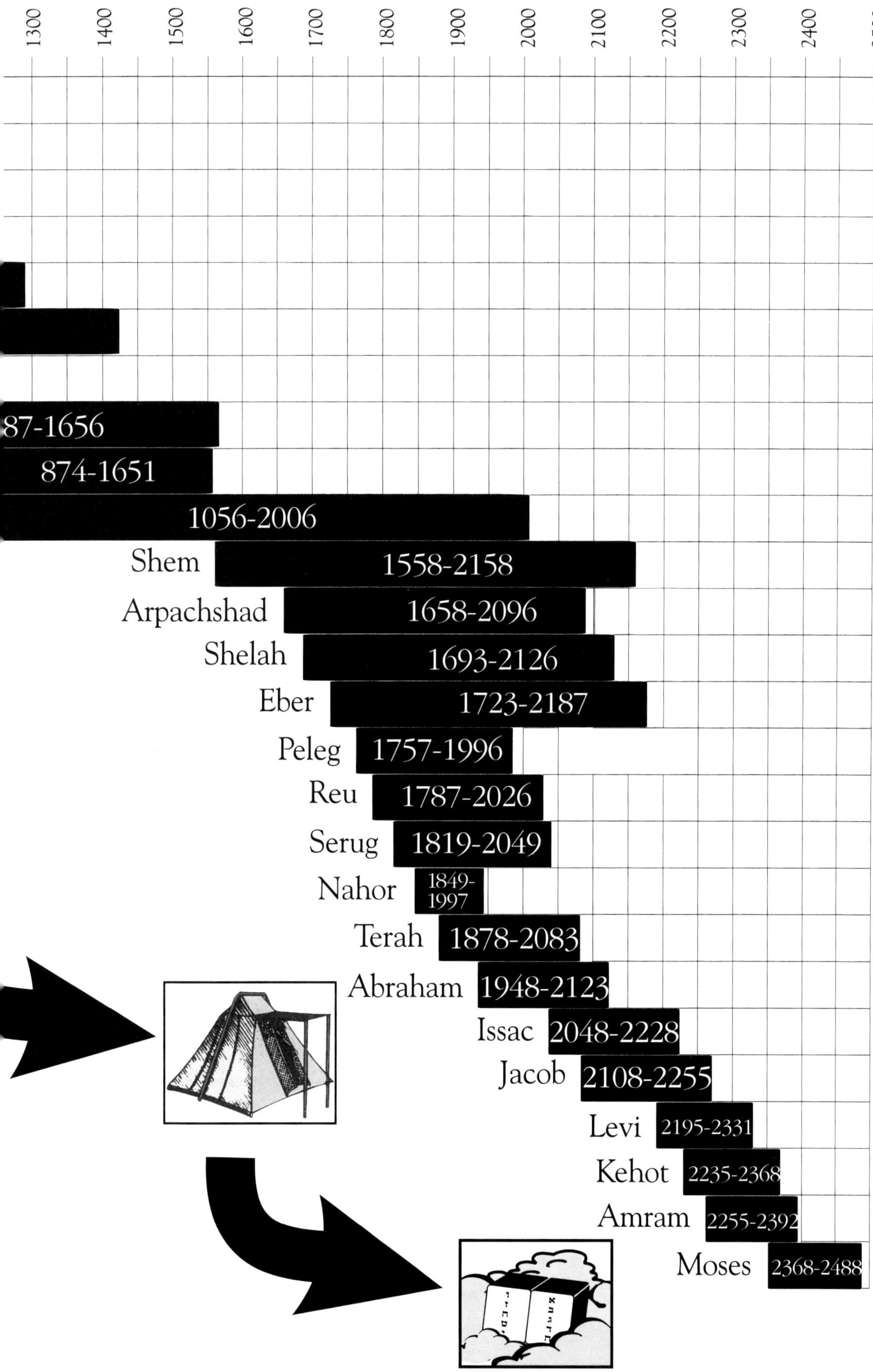
1300
1400
1500
1600
1700
1800
1900
2000
2100
2200
2300
2400
2500
87-1656
874-1651
1056-2006
Shem 1558-2158
Arpachshad 1658-2096
Shelah 1693-2126
Eber 1723-2187
Peleg 1757-1996
Reu 1787-2026
Serug 1819-2049
Nahor 1849-1997
Terah 1878-2083
Abraham 1948-2123
Issac 2048-2228
Jacob 2108-2255
Levi 2195-2331
Kehot 2235-2368
Amram 2255-2392
Moses 2368-2488

הוצאת ספרים
קרני הוד תורה
קה"ת
ליובאוויטש